introspection
ellie halo

allow this book
to take you on a journey
to deeper self awareness
& reclaiming your true essence

this is an ode to my younger self;
and the women who came before me
and the women who walk beside me

you are light.
you are loved.
you are enough.

the surrender
the healing
the expansion

the surrender

ellie halo

why can't you just love me?

- the bathroom mirror

introspection

carved out red lines
against my hip crease
aching to feel something
other than hopelessness

a destructive ritual
reflecting in the mirror
as an act of self preservation

this blade drew roadmaps
between lonely nights
and sorrowing sentiments
until the ink ran out
leaving trace marks
for tomorrow's pain

ellie halo

*dear body, i am sorry
for how i punished you
when you were just
trying to survive.*

*you deserve better.
i vow to do better.*

introspection

we hide in closets
to repress the suffering
that takes residence
in our bones

creating friction
against the walls
of our skin
bursting
at the brink
seeping crimson
through the cracks

ellie halo

*pain is inevitable,
suffering is optional.
come out of hiding,
show the world
your battle scars.*

introspection

i wish that i could have been
your saving grace

when parts of your identity
became mass amongst gravity
falling to the pits of your heartache

i wish that i could have known
that the darkness of grief followed you
and clung to your empty sheets
as the sun rose and retreat

i wish that i could have held you
when you fell into hysteria
on the kitchen floor
gasping through shallow breaths

i wish i could have saved you
from the internalised misery
that suffocated you constantly
from being left for another

ellie halo

i wish i could have told you
that your heart would learn
to love again

not another;
but no other
than the only one
who truly deserves
your heart

because the love of your life
was you, and was always you
right from the start

- words that never made it to my mother

introspection

grazed knuckles
held against his throat
teaching him violence
is the only solution
to a man's heartache

if only you taught him
the strength in vulnerability
or the power of empathy

ellie halo

when you walked away
you left a blazing inferno
shaped like a child
trapped in a six foot two figure
raging like wildfire

screams of terror
and bottled up tears
were never enough
to calm the flames

introspection

the kindle keeps
his trauma warm
and when a breeze
comes through
after the fourth whisky
on a stormy afternoon
he reignites

see men are taught
to fight fire with fire
without learning how
to put the flames out

ellie halo

*we must open space for our men
to release the pain they carry
like boulders on their backs
from years of being taught
to hide their vulnerability.*

*watch just how beautiful
a man can really be
when he sheds his ego
and steps back into his soul.*

introspection

the dinner table
silenced my cries
the cutting edge of bitterness
sharper than a steak knife
your disappointment
spilled across the pine
lips quivering with anger
as you take a sip of wine
if only i had been quiet
and did what i was told
obedience is unobtainable
at only eleven years old

ellie halo

– be seen not heard

introspection

i witnessed the manifestation
of destructive communication
for years on end

convinced that love
was a made up notion
that fell apart
in slow motion
like a movie
stuck on replay

love with conditions
leads to broken promises
or a hand against the oesophagus
suffocating till death
do us part

i am no longer
young and naive
i do not believe
in fairytale endings

ellie halo

what did love look like to you growing up?

introspection

for a hopeless pisces
to find resistance
in believing that marriage
is anything other
than a permission slip
or a cruel cage of restriction
is a poetic tragedy

ellie halo

what are your beliefs on marriage?

who and what has shaped these beliefs?

introspection

a faulty distinguisher
found in the ashes
of a house fire

a fatal destruction
caused by red rage
and a carried down gene
of an irreversible temper

charcoal stained cloth
mirroring chest to chest
eyes locked like lasers
meeting in the dark sky

ellie halo

there is no backing down
from a family dispute
admitting defeat
will strip you bare
from your armour
and pride

- *a family firestorm*

introspection

when you chose to be
a father to a new comer
over your own
you gave me evidence
to support the narrative
that a man could never stay

my own blood
exhausted
by my brokenness

how could it be
that the only man
i have ever truly loved
did not want me

ellie halo

when in your childhood did you feel unworthy of love?

how can you heal these parts of you?

introspection

silence rings
alarms in my skull
please say something
anything
before you go

ellie halo

i found answers in your silence.

introspection

violet blooms
drowning in matter
perched against
the window cill

you haven't called in weeks

i replay our last conversation
both bitter and sweet
you care for my safety
but never about my dreams

for just once
i wish you would value
my happiness
over my success

ellie halo

i bite my tongue
as i hold back tears
dialling the 8 digits
that connect me to you

nine minutes
and twenty three seconds
is all it takes
to empty my throat
of meaningless words
and to fulfil a duty
that was long overdue

introspection

i avoid the darkness
by being the torch for others
basking in the glory
of escapism

ellie halo

what are you distracting yourself from by giving all of your energy to others?

introspection

my eyes are stuck
in black and white viewing
seeing the world
in gradients and shades
but never in the vast colours
of the rainbow

the paradox:
of both simplicity and complexity
existing in the same space
begs of me to go inwards
drawing the curtains
retreating back to darkness
where it feels safe
to introduce light
at my own accord

but what if today
i opened myself up
to seeing it all –
feeling it all?

would i feel abundant?
would i feel scarce?
or would i just feel it all?

ellie halo

i open myself up
to see the world in colour –
i no longer want to hide away
from experiencing life
in its fullest capacity.

introspection

an impulsive purchase
of an aeroplane ticket
accompanied by
a pool of tears

the two components
of my escape route

freedom chaser

hooks
sunk into my back
pulling me
in every direction
except the one
in which
i wanted to go

ellie halo

what are you running from?

introspection

i feel homesick
yet i do not know
where home is

ellie halo

home: _____

introspection

i live in a world
with twelve seasons
where i cannot stand
stagnancy

or is it just
that i am irritable
itching to move on
to see the world
or fill a void

i cannot stop
this burning in my chest
this unsettling need
for change

i pack my bags
and rid my belongings
until i'm left with nothing
but a compulsion
to run

ellie halo

every time
i get lost wondering
am i running forward
or backwards?

introspection

somedays
i search
for something
more

like i have been drinking
out of an empty cup

the whole world
is before me
offering up abundance
and yet
i still feel scarce

ellie halo

*when you subtract
gratitude from the equation
you are left with nothing.*

turn what you have into enough.

introspection

when the dopamine drops
you will finally see
that no amount of fame
or digits in your bank account
will make you happy

do not waste
your precious life
chasing boastful boys
or instagram likes

happiness
is not external validation
it is a fleeting moment
an indescribable sensation
that comes from true connection
and constant affirmation

it's time for you
to start living your truth
let go of what
no longer serves you

ellie halo

who and what are you glorifying?

introspection

the pounding embedded
beneath my chest
suffocates me rapidly
until air becomes as scarce
as water in a desert
leaving me thirsting
for tranquility

ellie halo

what thoughts are making you anxious?

how can you self-soothe?

breathe in
1, 2, 3

breathe out
1, 2, 3

introspection

vision in a haze
staring blankly
at the white washed walls

ruminating thoughts
move in motion
running marathons
in my mind

the notion of failure
writing profanities
up and down my arms
exposing my weakness
to the world

no one warns you
about the torment that comes
with repetitive defeat
and a shattered dream

ellie halo

are you letting your perceived failures keep you stagnant or stuck?

introspection

the city rush
the blank faces
the hum of traffic
soften my sorrows

knowing
that it is safe
for me to seek
refuge here
no one can see me
for i blend in
amongst the crowd

another human
with scars and stories
that remain untold

ellie halo

what's your story?

introspection

don't lose your spark
in the darkness of a screen
life is happening
outside your phone

ellie halo

put your phone down.
take a walk. look up.
there is beauty all around you.

introspection

self depreciation:
the joker's mask

a shield
that deflects
the truth

the sharpness
of her words
cuts the silence
in half

an attempt
to find confirmation
in her bias
as if the world
sees her flaws
before her beauty

ellie halo

what insecurities do you cover up with self depreciation?

how can you empower yourself and improve your self talk?

introspection

just when i thought
i had left you behind
you came to visit
at the dinner table
creating chaos
between my fork
and conscience

you visited again
when i was brushing my teeth
washing away the guilt
from the food i had eaten

you showed up unannounced
to my birthday party
force feeding me vodka on ice
when all i wanted
was to dance with champagne

you barged in during intimacy
whispering words of repulsion
up and down my spine
begging of me
to turn the lights off

ellie halo

*our minds can be so cruel.
block out the monster
that lives within you
telling you that your worth
is determined by your weight.*

*come back to your heart.
your truth can always be found there.*

introspection

i don't want to be seen
for my exterior
which hides away
my heart

i want to be seen
for my tender soul
and the way i make
people feel

if only they could see
that the shape of my body
is the least interesting
thing about me

ellie halo

i am more than my appearance.

introspection

insanity
feels like grieving
someone who visits you
every time you close your eyes

insanity
looks like waiting
for the perfect time
to take a leap and dive

insanity
sounds like despising
the very thing
that keeps you alive

ellie halo

what is driving you insane?

introspection

my relationship with death
is three times removed
i am disconnected
from the truth of it all

boundless seas
keep me from facing
the reality of loss

avoidance
feels better than
the heaviness
of grief

ellie halo

grief feels like _____

introspection

starvation
manipulation
lack of sensation
born into a generation
who finds no hesitation
in relishing in instant gratification

ellie halo

don't be the person they expect you to be.

introspection

the words are trapped
on the roof of my mouth
aching to be unleashed
overgrown and decayed
sinking holes
in my ruby red flesh
pressed against
skin and cheek

profanities
pulling at my lips
biting my tongue
down in despair

a lady never spills her secrets
or shares her disapproval
beyond her breath

so
i smile
politely

ellie halo

what words are you repressing?

introspection

my safety plan
spread between knuckles
in the shape of car keys

danger breathing
down my neck
rocking my head
side to side
like a ventriloquist

girls should not walk alone at night
or wear short skirts
that tempt the male gaze
and don't wear headphones!
are you trying to get killed?
stairwells
lead to dead ends
take the elevator
avoid conversation
don't use your phone
or catch the bus after dark
stay vigilant
don't talk to strangers
close your legs
be polite
cover up
behave

and just
stay out of trouble

ellie halo

*the responsibility
of creating a world
where we are free from fear
for simply existing in a female body
should not fall on the shoulders
of our young girls.*

*as a collective
we should be devoting practice
to dismantling the entitlement
of the patriarchy.*

introspection

you locked the bathroom door
behind our drunken bodies
to stop an intervention
to a crime you felt entitled to make

my slurred speech
or quivering hands
did not interrupt you
from taking control

my attempt to escape
the caving walls
and heavy dew
did not phase you
or your hunger
to have it your way

only now
at twenty three
can i truly see
what you have done to me

ellie halo

i let you go
a long time ago
but still i carry
the weight of you

introspection

i sought comfort
in the arms of another
which only prolonged
the healing

soon enough
the band aids fell off
and the wounds
remained the same

ellie halo

what are you distracting yourself from dealing with?

introspection

when i hear your name
i cannot refrain
from tensing up inside

my body is rejecting you
cleansing the residue
of your destruction

they say it takes seven years
for every cell in your body
to regenerate

this gives me hope
that the parts of you
that lay dormant in my blood
will slowly fade
overtime

ellie halo

my body is purging your touch.
i am reclaiming my own anatomy.
you are no longer welcome here.

introspection

i carry the burden
of legs and breasts
attracting the attention
of the voyeur

i curl my shoulders
and tug at my skirt
finding discomfort
in my own presence

my eyes do not unlock
from the pavement
for catching a glare
makes *me* feel shame
for the parts of my existence
that have been claimed
by everyone else
but me

ellie halo

my body has been sexualised
and opened up for discussion
without desire or consent

the male gaze
stains my body
like a bad rash
i cannot remove

introspection

i feel dirty
for simply existing
impure
in a skinsuit
of a woman

when i'm alone
naked in my own eye
i try to rid the guilt
with soap and water
but still
i wrap myself
in shame

ellie halo

how has the male gaze impacted your relationship with your body?

introspection

swallowing syllables
purging pain
revealing politeness
holding shame
a wild woman
leashed and tamed
is a prisoner
in society's cage

ellie halo

*unbind yourself
from the internalised misogyny.
you weren't put on this earth
to play small.
break out of the cage
& make something of yourself.*

introspection

'have you found a boyfriend yet?'
a desperate sense of hope
rolling off their tongues
accompanied
with a gentle pat
of condolence
on the shoulder

they shame us
through pitying dialogue
'don't worry, you'll find someone one day!'

as if my life's mission
is to find a man
who will get down
on one knee

ellie halo

my relationship status
does not define who i am
i do not need a man
to validate my existence.

introspection

poisonous narratives
dominated the television screen
programming our adolescent minds

to see—

mistreatment
a form of flattery

lack of boundaries
a*n expression of admiration*

"no thank you"
translates to
"please do"

a subconscious accumulation
of stories that confirm the notion
that we are simply here
to please and perform

ellie halo

what were you conditioned to believe about your role in society through media?

introspection

i create disappointment
by carving out
a heart shaped pedestal
demanding the ones i admire
to take a seat
with a blindfold on

i orchestrate their impact
choosing to perceive them
through a rose tinted lens
that fits within my ideals

until one day
they escape the throne
sprinting through the wilderness
as i chase their shadow
with wide open arms
and a desire to be loved
the way i always dreamed of

ellie halo

who are you putting on a pedestal?

*how are your unrealistic expectations
impacting your relationships?*

introspection

my heart breaks a little
every time you leave

they say distance
makes the heart grow fonder
but baby my heart is aching
for you

ellie halo

who is your heart longing for?

introspection

broken promises
empty words
forgotten birthdays
cancelled plans
texts left on read
late night arguments
months of misery

ellie halo

*let go of people
who do not value
your time and energy.*

introspection

i speak with sincerity
you speak with your fingers
crossed behind your back

ellie halo

- pathological liar

introspection

my dignity left me
when i laid there lifeless
as you ignored my tears
valuing your pleasure
over my pain

my voice lost its power
when my needs met rolling eyes
palms pressed against your ears
like a selfish child

my heart cried for you
when you rejected my love
to play it cool
in front of the guys

ellie halo

my hope diminished
when at the end of it all
i asked if you still loved me
and you replied
i don't know

introspection

i could tell you
about all the times
you made my eyes wilt
and sting with sorrow

but today
i don't feel like wasting
my breath

ellie halo

so instead
i will leave you
with unspoken words
and drown you
in silence

introspection

imprisoned
by his potential
dreaming
of what could be

still
like a body
of water

drowning
in midnight
poison

words spoken
from deep
desperation

ellie halo

an attempt to fix
shattered glass
using hot glue
and words
that lost their value
upon repetition

piecing together
a million
shattered
segments

but darling don't you see?

you cannot fix
a mess you did not make.

introspection

when your friends found me
crying my eyes out for you
over a gin and tonic
on the dance floor
they told me to let you go

it turns out
i was too blind to see
that everyone else
saw the real you
except me

ellie halo

are you choosing to ignore the signs?

introspection

you cannot save him;

you can only save yourself
from the emotional distress
that paints your eyelids
black and blue

when you try to save someone
who plays the role
of villain and victim
you both don't make it
in the end

ellie halo

words for my younger self–

*do not fall in love
with someone's potential
of who they could be.*

introspection

i take the scenic route home
every time our song comes on
just so i can cry
more tears over you

ellie halo

– driving in a rainstorm

introspection

our bodies intertwined
while our troublesome past
runs circles in my mind

how did i end up here?
laying in your bed
it must have been something
witty that you said

i tell my friends
you're dead to me
until its 1am
and i need you to breathe

when does it stop?
this manipulation and spite
my heart is heavy
weeping under the moonlight

ellie halo

what was once love
replaced by fear

*how could i ever live
without you my dear?*

introspection

your skin like fire
hot to touch
lips like candy
sweet as such
your words are venom
leaving wounds to heal
you trace my curves
nothing left to reveal
your body on mine
creating heat
until you up and leave
i'm begging you please
please don't leave

ellie halo

*laying with an ex lover
will never satisfy your need for intimacy.
come back home to yourself
and sit with your feelings.
you are all you need.*

introspection

2am terrors
waking up to torrential tears
trickling down my cheeks

i had a dream
you were right here with me
and i woke to a nightmare
of empty sheets
and a cold pillow

ellie halo

i am relearning how to be alone.
time will heal this emptiness within me.

introspection

when the moon
swallows the stars
with its obnoxiously
blinding shine

ellie halo

*i remember–
i am not yours
and you are not mine.*

introspection

i cannot have you
circulating my blood
while i muster up the courage
to lay with another
and create new memories
that paint over you

ellie halo

how can you heal your past sexual trauma?

introspection

my boyfriends
became my dictators

my self worth
found dependency
in their terms
and conditions

a story
of submission
and sacrifice
repetitive trauma
and deteriorating
self esteem

ellie halo

*don't lose your worth
in the presence of another.
break free from relationships
that teach you in order to be worthy
you must compress and conform
to their expectations.*

introspection

you robbed me
in broad daylight
shoving my sanity
into your backpack
then you found me
hiding in the closet
yet you did not care to run
when the police arrived
they could not find evidence
of the damage
that had been done

you shook hands with them
winning them over
with your endearing charm
no one but me
could hear the sirens
of the pounding security alarm

ellie halo

how could i be
the only one who could see
that you stole my dignity
and left me empty

- the memoirs of a narcissist

introspection

i close my eyelids at 11:11
and say a prayer
for you

laying wide awake
tossing and turning
with passive insomnia

your pain is mine
and that is the curse
of deeply felt empathy

ellie halo

*i'm freeing myself from emotions
that are not mine to carry.
moving forward,
i will consciously protect my energy.*

introspection

i was seeking solace
in the familiarity of you

my heart knew
that you would break me
again and again and again

but still
i found my way
back to your arms

i waited for you
to speak words of comfort
but you did not care
about my fragility

you waited for me
to say you were right
but i did not care
about your ego

ellie halo

– always running back to you

introspection

seasonal love
carved out conditions
you give me your heart
to only take it back
when the storm rolls in

ellie halo

- forever love is a lie

introspection

hues of violet
paint the sky
you stand there lifeless
watching me cry
stone cold skin
silence is your reply
my love is empty
you took the last supply

ellie halo

say you'll try
even if it's a lie
because tonight
i will die
if i get on that plane
and fly
without a proper
goodbye

introspection

fifteen thousand
one hundred and sixty
kilometres away
from you

yet

i can still hear
you whispering me
goodnight

- 12:13 am

ellie halo

when the stars shine, who is on your mind?

introspection

the ache in my chest
longs for your presence
if i could just stand
in an empty room with you
i would feel full
again

ellie halo

find the parts of you
that feel empty without their presence
& fill them with self love.
you are whole, just as you are.

introspection

i hold my breath
waiting for butterflies
in the pit of my stomach
to break free from their cocoon
only for them to be still-born
decaying in the core of me

wishful thinking
and romanticising life
always leaves me
with a graveyard inside

ellie halo

are your expectations leading you to repetitive disappointment?

introspection

the sun won't wait for you
to shed your final tears
and pick yourself up
off the bathroom floor

it will keep rising
and falling
on schedule

days become weeks
weeks become months
and one day
will become the day
that the sun
will rise and fall
and for once
the memory of him
will not haunt you

ellie halo

*find little moments of joy
to distract you from the heaviness
of grieving lost love.*

the healing

ellie halo

with shame
comes malnourishment
of the mind, body and soul

introspection

i remind myself
of the suffering
that replaced the lost numbers
on the bathroom scale

i remind myself
that the biggest gain
was getting my freedom back

i remind myself
that i am enough
no matter my mass
amongst gravity

i am returning home
to the place of my creation
my body is boundlessly beautiful
and deeply worthy of love

ellie halo

*i am claiming my life back.
i crave freedom —
to live in this body
without punishment
or restriction.*

introspection

i draw love hearts
on the shower screen door
leaving a note of adoration
for when i return
and undress in the mirror
feeling vulnerable
about the parts of me
that i am yet to make peace with

the small notion
of a shape representing love
reminds me to stop being so silly
wasting precious time
picking apart my reflection
when i could just simply change
my perception

ellie halo

*change your inner dialogue
by shifting from negative thoughts
to positive affirmations.
your mind is a powerful healer.
use it to your advantage.*

introspection

reclaim your power
return home within
your body was always yours

never meant to be taken
by the hands of the oppressor

never meant to be told
how to dress up or down

never meant to be starved
by beauty standards

never meant to be shamed
by the natural cycles of life

your body
will always be yours
even when it feels like its not;

ellie halo

come home to your body
speak to it with kindness
dress it with conviction
move it with intuition
share it with empowerment
hold it with compassion
treat it with love

it is yours
& only yours

introspection

recovery is not linear
or absent of relapse

it is a conscious decision
that your future
is more important
than giving into a rush
of euphoria

find praise
for the small wins
and compassion
in the fall backs
to find peace
in the journey

ellie halo

what does recovery look like to you?

can you find pride in how far you have come on this journey?

introspection

self constraint
is a slow death
of your souls mission
to be here now
completely wild
and free

ellie halo

what are you restricting yourself from?

introspection

as you take your last breaths
laying beside yellow tulips
laced in best wishes

you will finally see
that your weight
and your mistakes
did not make the cut
of your remembrance

you will be celebrated
in ways that honour
the way you made
people light up

do not waste your time
on what will not
make it to your grave

ellie halo

*you have one life.
do not waste it getting caught up
in things that will lose significance
on your last day on earth.*

*pour your energy
into living in alignment
with what your soul came here to do.*

introspection

we are taught
to bypass ourselves;
that being selfless
is admirable

in retrospect
being selfless
is simply
leaving less
for yourself

less freedom
less excitement
less time
less energy
less love

ellie halo

see yourself in the flowers
they lustre with light
when they are nurtured
with warmth and devotion

the more you tend to them
the more they grow
the more they bloom

introspection

seeking external approval
builds on the belief
that validation is a remedy
for low self worth

when truth be told
your own endorsement
will set you free
from the restraints
of another's envy

ellie halo

whose approval are you seeking?

introspection

judgement and hatred
reveals the bitterness
you hold within yourself
towards yourself

these parts of you
are being called to
burst open and heal
growing roots
creating space
for your awakening

ellie halo

*do not let the bitter taste of revenge
conquer the sweetness of integrity.*

*allow yourself
to reject ego-driven action
and charge yourself
with humility and compassion.*

introspection

i spent years hating you
scared to open my heart to you
terrified of talking to you

i must have forgotten
about that time you held my hand
skipping down the pavement
oblivious to anything other
than the smile on my face

i must have thrown out
every birthday card
you wrote with sincerity
signed with lots of love

i must have erased
you holding me in your arms
when my heart broke into pieces
for the very first time

ellie halo

today i am thankful
for discovering the art
of forgiveness

for i cannot live
without a father
with a heart like yours

introspection

when you chose
to abandon your existence
here on earth
we were robbed
of so much more
than the function
of your organs

we lost the familiar smile
that carried us through blizzards
keeping us warm in the winter snow

ellie halo

i guess i feel selfish
for failing to understand
your decision to depart
when your suffering
was bigger than me
bigger than us

i hope you found
the solitude you were seeking
finding a place to rest
your tired eyes
amongst the night sky

R.I.P

introspection

bleak afternoons
dreary eyed gaze
waking up without hope
i tell myself
'this is just a phase'

ignoring text messages
my cognition feels hazy
my body isn't functioning
or am i just being lazy?

i have too much time
to reflect on the past
on days like today
it all feels so dark

when my mind forgets
how to adapt with optimism
i need space to feel
to tune in and listen

a storm feels all encompassing
until the skies clear with blue
it's only then you can feel
the warmth inside of you

ellie halo

tomorrow or the next
your shadows will begin to fade
the darkness will slowly dissipate
and you will no longer be afraid

allow the rainfall
to wash away
the heaviness
of yesterday

introspection

tears are a form of healing
that compress your suffering
into crystallised raindrops

a chemical reaction
to pent up emotions
trickling translucent spheres
down your rubicund cheeks

when the heaviness of your jaw
starts to loosen grip
the salty waves
will wash over
your pain

it is only then
the true healing
can begin

ellie halo

allow yourself to shed.
drop deep into the pit of your stomach
and let it all gush out.
tears are not a sign of weakness,
they are proof that you are healing.

introspection

when your heart
gets ripped out of you
bleeding out
into your sheets

ellie halo

surrender.
go deeper.
love harder.

introspection

i run my fingers
over your arms
seeking answers
to unasked questions
like there are words
to be found in your veins

ellie halo

what questions are you not asking?

introspection

i love until
there is nothing left to give
offering up
my entire existence
in exchange for the heat
of your body against mine

ellie halo

how much of yourself are you giving to another person?

introspection

i could pour you
honey and lemon
in the light hours
of dusk and dawn

i would do anything
to keep you smiling
even when the sun is blinding
and our bodies are fighting
for distance and space

because in the deep darkness
you are my saving grace

ellie halo

these romance novels have taught me
that to love with passion
you must sacrifice it all.

i lost myself in you.

i am learning to differentiate
love and codependency.

introspection

how am i
supposed to separate
lust and love
when both taste the same
on your lips

ellie halo

– lost in the moment

introspection

there are holes
on the brink of my heart
leaking out
into my bloodstream
turning my veins
into a runway
for immense love
and pain

you tell me
you don't understand
why i love so hard
when i know the pain
will hit just as hard
but you don't see
that this is just
my biology

ellie halo

— *leaky heart*

introspection

how do i let go of him
without hating
hearing his name
or driving myself
completely insane?

i still smile
when his name lights up my phone
or when i put on his oversized shirt
that drowns my aching bones
his face paints the walls
of my voiceless empty home
the walls are caving
as i sit all alone
waiting
by the phone
for his ringtone

ellie halo

how do you fix a broken heart?

introspection

i wish i could hate you
but truth be told
when i look at you
all i see is a garden of roses

ellie halo

*you make loving easy
and hating ten times harder.*

introspection

in a moment of weakness
i allowed my ego to take over
holding me under water
until a rapid sense of validation
bubbled to the surface

i forgot that your approval
is not the lifeline i need

ellie halo

*the key component to self soothing
is validating your own emotions.*

introspection

someone
who makes you question
your desirability in the darkness

does not deserve
to witness your glory
in the midst of the summer sun

ellie halo

*you are not too much
for asking to be loved
in your entirety.*

introspection

you taught me lessons
that no textbook could
breaking down my worth
so i could learn
to build it back up

never again
to be silenced by a man
who does not attempt
to make space for my voice
without interruptions
or condescending questions

a woman
with a wild roar
is the biggest threat to a man
who cannot dominate his prey

ellie halo

when has a man silenced your voice?

how can you reclaim your power?

introspection

i am healing
the wounds engraved
from the roughness
of many hands

i remind myself
your hands
are not theirs

ellie halo

*learning to trust again can be messy.
create a safe space for you to explore
what it feels like to be held with soft hands.*

introspection

skin and bones
pressed against fresh linen
tangled up
in one another's presence
you came to me
to teach me lessons
on how a man should be
while sharing space
beneath the sheets

your heart is beating fast
but your fingers are moving slow
the look in your eyes
makes my skin shiver and glow

your chest expands
as you hold my hands
and remind me of what
a man can be

ellie halo

*without respect, presence and consent
the magic of intimacy will diminish.*

wait for the magic.

introspection

i thank you
for acting as a mirror
reflecting the wounded child
that has yet been tended to
covered by steel-plated ego
hiding from the light

this darkness within me
seeks acceptance not dissonance

begging to be discovered
unfolding like a map
ready to be explored
by an open heart
and curiosity

ellie halo

*find reverence for situations
that trigger your inner child.
these special moments
shed light on what's calling
to be nurtured within.*

*hold her
& remind her
she is loved.*

introspection

i spent hours digging deep
into the dusty corners
of the patriarchal construct

revealing
the liberation
of this twisted union
between man
and woman

finding empowerment
in the opportunity
to recreate my beliefs
on romance and intimacy

the women
who fought for my freedom
applauding as i stand tall
on my own two feet

ellie halo

what outdated beliefs are you recreating?

introspection

release the discomfort
that seeks refuge
in the pit of your stomach
for the tribulations
that you have endured

thousands of miles
you've walked in trenches
knee deep in thick mud
your tired bones
pleading for stagnancy

despite your anguish
and restless limbs
you found resilience
amongst the resistance

do not let your triumphs
be repressed through modesty
or hindered by indignity
for you are a warrior
and a survivor

ellie halo

show the world your lionheart.

introspection

when you are stripped
from cloth and armour
baring your soul
naked and vulnerable
— run to the fire

choose recklessness over safety
choose integrity over what is easy
choose courage over fear

not because the flames
won't burn you
not because the heat
won't liquefy your heart
but because the ecstasy
of the hot and heavy
is medicine

ellie halo

how can you brave the fire?

introspection

forgiving
the deepest heartache
isn't about anyone else
but you,
the pain,
and the rising

ellie halo

who and what are you not allowing yourself to fully forgive?

introspection

an apology
for the one that needs it most;
my heart

i forgive myself
for being ashamed
of my own anatomy

i forgive myself
for not asking for help
when i needed it most

i forgive myself
for thinking that my success
would make me worthy
of my father's pride

i forgive myself
for being too busy
to pick up the phone and call
the one's who mean the most

ellie halo

i forgive myself
for feeling like a victim
and not recognising my privilege

i forgive myself
for punishing my body
for having an appetite

i forgive myself
for not seeing sex
as a sacred practice

i forgive myself
for finding comfort
in another woman's flaws

i forgive myself
for losing faith
in people who never
lost faith in me

introspection

i forgive myself
for not fully knowing
how to truly forgive.

your turn:

i forgive myself for....

introspection

i choose to trust
beyond what i can see
on the warped horizon
as an act of faith
in all that is yet to come

i trust in the way
my heart breaks a little
before the healing
can begin

i trust in the divine timing
of my deepest wishes
because the universe
has its own timeline

i trust in the knowing
of the rising after pain
because we need contrast
in order to fully come alive

i trust
again and again
even when proven
otherwise

ellie halo

how can you restore trust in knowing that everything is working in your highest favour?

introspection

when given a pen
and blank paper
she speaks
a poets dialect

ellie halo

what language does your soul speak?

introspection

we drove down
windy roads
spilling our hearts
out the open windows
your right palm
resting on my thigh
while future scenarios
play out in my mind
the salty breeze
kissing upon your cheek
i've been waiting for
this moment for weeks
dreaming of you
back here with me
taking adventures
out into the big blue sea

ellie halo

legs wrapped
around your waist
as my lips quiver
to get a taste
of what it's like
to fall in love again
you pull me close
and count to ten
we drop our bodies
under the crashing waves
washing away
the longing of yesterday

introspection

his eyes were not brown;
they were deep hazel
and burnt sage

seeping butter
and cinnamon
warm like honey
in the melting pot

they told stories
of nostalgia
keeping my body warm
in the perishing hours
of a dreary winter moon down

ellie halo

– to feel truly seen

introspection

my mind is awake
while my body lays in slumber
resting on yours
like it was made to carry
my silhouette
into the early morning
offering it up
at sunrise

shadows casted
kissing my hips
pulling you closer
back pressed up
against your lips

time slows down
when i'm in your presence
continuously mesmerised
by your pure essence

ellie halo

intimacy
is more than touch
it's a feeling of devotion
to exchanging mutual trust

a space for one another
to be accepted and seen
for the anguish and the expansion
and all that lies between

introspection

my body is not a graveyard
it is a lavender field
in the middle of spring

ellie halo

i will love this body.
i will accept this body.
i will respect this body.

introspection

i was taught
that the emptiness
on the right side of my bed
should make my eyes leak

but somehow,
it reminds me
that the warmth
of my own skin
is enough of a lullaby
to cradle me to sleep

ellie halo

i am reclaiming my own love.
i am full without you here with me.

introspection

as i recreate
the concept of intimacy
i find peace in my sobriety

the child within me
screaming for attention
is no longer being fed
instant gratification
and validation
by a man's presence

she is being tended to
with love and grace,
compassion and awareness,
vulnerability and depth

ellie halo

i am alone
but i am not lonely

- an affirmation of my truth

the expansion

ellie halo

i had to fall out of love
to fall back in love
with myself

introspection

waking from slumber
to the familiar call
of a satin bowerbird
and an empty home
reminds me
of my fullness

residue of lavender
weaved in between the linen
calming my mind
as the light pours in
casting rainbows
upon my bare chest

ellie halo

slow mornings
have become a ritual
of deep self love and surrender

introspection

i swapped drinking poison
with milky hot cacao
and late night taxi rides
with sunset conversations

i redirected my focus
from boys to books
and aesthetics to authenticity
the veil was lifting
and i could not go back

comfort over trends
self validation instead of gratification
healing over void filling

maybe's replaced by no's
kindness conquering critique
and for once in my life
i felt free from expectation
from the external world
to be anything other
than myself

ellie halo

what changes need to be made for you to thrive as your most authentic self?

introspection

soften
to find strength

sit in stillness
to create movement

ellie halo

stand in chaos
to obtain inner peace

empty your cup
to feel full again

introspection

strawberry skies
and a half cut moon
stained my vision
one spring afternoon
as i sit alone
on the overhanging cliff
i peer across the bay
into the cloudy abyss

a presence so pure
taking weight
from my bones
i have finally let go
of trying to control
the unknown

ellie halo

release to renew
a concept so simple
yet so profoundly true

when we come back
to the home of our heart
we find peace
amongst the madness
just like
abstract art

introspection

i refuse to
shift and shape
into anything
that doesn't feel
like freedom

ellie halo

what does freedom feel like to you?

introspection

windows down
beats blaring
hair a mess
dancing in the wind
salt on skin
wet nylon
hugging my hips
sunset creeping through
the mountain tops
kissing my forehead
through dusty glass
appreciation
pinching at my cheeks
punching holes
on either side
causing my eyes
to replay the motion
of the high tide

ellie halo

alive.
the feeling evoked
by living through a lens
of pure love
and reckless trust
that every moment
is worth living for

introspection

i will no longer
care for the size
that labels the fabric
covering my skin

ellie halo

– dressing room breakthroughs

introspection

absence
of appreciation
for the home
of your soul
is a curse
sent by society

rise to the challenge
to love yourself completely
without conditions or bounds

the rebirth
of a wild woman
who has mastered the gift
of love for self
is a beautiful threat
to this world

ellie halo

how can you show appreciation for your authentic beauty?

introspection

i took a vow
to love the parts of me
that i thought were unlovable
because even if
i can't find their beauty
they still deserve
to be worshiped like god

ellie halo

*make a promise to yourself
that you will work towards
loving every inch of your being.*

introspection

the bees flirting
with the daisies
on a tuesday afternoon
make my cheeks
soften and shine
in awe

ellie halo

*she does not wait
for people to admire her beauty.
she keeps making art,
because she is art.*

introspection

i love myself
unconditionally

not for my physicality
or my external reality
but what lies beneath
this cloth and bone

ellie halo

what does unconditional self love look like to you?

introspection

i laid my tired limbs
across the back of your car
you sat in the front
peering over the head rest
with stardust in your eyes

*"take me to a time where you
felt pure happiness"*

my frown dissipated
through storytelling
and deep belly laughs

a keepsake
that joy is all you need
on a seedy sunday afternoon

ellie halo

*travel back to a time
you felt pure happiness –
what made that moment so special?*

introspection

my feet find comfort
amongst the muddy tufts of grass
that take the weight
of my sorrows

my bones are heavy
sinking towards
the steaming soil

the heat of the earth
dancing around my ankles
restoring my roots

i find peace
when i'm at one
with you

ellie halo

*i feel fully held
when my feet are connected
to mother earth.
when life feels like
it's running circles around you
kick your shoes off & plant your feet
back where they belong.*

introspection

elderflower and sparkling tonic
swimming in crushed ice
surrounded by sunflowers
and subtle scents of vanilla
the breeze sends shivers
down my sunken spine
serendipity stains
my curious wandering mind
dreaming of another world
where only love exists
i get so easily lost
in my internal abyss

ellie halo

where do your day dreams take you?

introspection

i sometimes wonder
if the backed up traffic jam
and the long queue at the petrol station
are simply signs to slow down

maybe without
the mundane hold ups
we would miss out
on the magic moments
that follow

ellie halo

learn tolerance.
learn patience.
learn presence.

introspection

our heartfelt vulnerabilities
shared over lemon cake
and blueberry jam

sun kissed cheeks
smiling sincerely
at the simplicity
of shared secrets

we talk about our future
and the life we will create
holding each others' vision
with glistening eyes of faith

you are me
and i am you
that is the beauty of sisterhood
that will always see us through

ellie halo

*my dearest friend
you make me believe
that true love still exists.*

introspection

i am worthy
of receiving boundless love
i surrender to the divinity
of the unknown timeline
and trust the unfolding
of the fruits of my labour

i hold space for myself
to retreat and renew
through self evaluation
and an unwavering commitment
to choose love
every single time

ellie halo

you are inherently worthy.

introspection

this morning
i twisted my torso
back and forth
shedding tension
accumulated
through dusk

i caught a glimpse
of my silhouette
staring back at me
through honest glass

for once
i found beauty
dented into texture
woven into stripes
marked upon my skin

i saw artistry
moulded into sculpture
worthy of admiration
from the creator
and the spectator

ellie halo

i made a vow
to frame this art
on the walls
of my tainted heart

showing appreciation
for it daily
through words of affirmation
and gestures of tenderness

after all
this art was created
just for me

it would be a crime
to refuse to find
love for this profound
mastery

introspection

i feel most alive
when i am upside down

competing
with gravity
challenging
the narrative
releasing
resistance
removing
the heavy armour
returning
to my child self

ellie halo

life is exhilarating
when my feet
are to the stars
and my hands
are on the ground

introspection

a full moon ritual
shared amongst the potency
of deeply conscious humans
and a desire for connection

filling our heart space
with intentions and forgiveness
releasing unwanted thoughts
and calling in a new found capacity
for radical self confidence

we exchange our rawest realisations
and hold space for each other
to breathe into the pain and suffering
we have endured in this phase

we embrace our wildest aspirations
and help manifest the collective energy
to elevate to the highest frequency
of our own potential

ellie halo

it is so deeply captivating
sharing our truth in safety
vulnerability is a binding force
that reminds us of our similarities
rather than our differences

when the moon beams
at its fullest volume
honour all that is
and trust the unfolding

introspection

warm sundowns
treading through liquid gold
waking up
in a lucid dream

i feel weightless
free from the heaviness
nothing is how
it once had seemed

ellie halo

— *dreaming with my eyes wide open*

introspection

i am redefining
my idea of success
i no longer aspire to be
the richest person in the room
i just want to be
the kindest

ellie halo

how do you define success?

introspection

my throat seized up
when you spoke words of venom

a request–
from my higher self
to take the sting away
with devotion
to understanding you
and your triggers

the most dangerous poison
you can ever swallow
is one-sided blame

ellie halo

*it is not me against you
it is us against the problem.*

introspection

i chose forgiveness
for the deepest of betrayals
not as an act of defeat
but as an act of healing

ellie halo

*a heart full of resentment
cannot be receptive to repairment.*

introspection

i am here
to feel the depths
of boundless love
in the space connecting
earth and sky
and everything
in between

my duty here
is to bow in honour
at life itself
and the magic
that lights me up
with inspiration
to be the best
i can be

ellie halo

*how can you drop into deeper alignment
with your highest self?*

introspection

the sunlight peaks
through arching palms
kissing my forehead
softening my frown
cheeks painted
like cherries
inviting my dimples
to come out
and play

ellie halo

i soften with the rising of the sun.

introspection

give me your entirety
and i will soften
like a sun-ripened peach
waiting to be devoured

sweet and sour seeping
around your supple lips
every shade of blush
emerging upon your cheeks
once you have me in your hands
i will stay sweet
for you

ellie halo

– falling for you

introspection

we pulled over
on the side of the road
jumping out
to snap sugar cane
carving up sweet sap
tongues soaked
in sucrose

ellie halo

the hum of cicadas composed
an unforgettable melody
so now when i drive
down these country roads
all i can think about
is how sweet your lips
taste at midnight

introspection

walking backwards
down the beachfront
with your finger tips
laced between mine

you look so wonderful
when you're lit up
by the moonlight

ellie halo

– losing track of time

introspection

i want to remember
the sensation
of your tongue at sunset
slow dancing
upon my neck

i want to remember
the stare
of your sapphire spheres
when i undress
in candle light luminance

i want time
to move slowly
so i can soak up
all of you

ellie halo

*fall in love with anything
that sparks a flame
in the fire of your soul.*

introspection

the space in between
is where i feel the most

ellie halo

press pause.
breathe into your heart space.
this moment matters.

introspection

dirt road wandering
yellow fire
casting shadows
against your back

my hand wrapped
around your pinky finger
pulling you with me
to chase the dragonflies
that dance circles
around our electric bodies

ellie halo

– i could walk this road for hours with you

introspection

heartbreak
again
and again
makes me feel
so fucking alive

ellie halo

my heart was built to break.
my heart was built to heal.
i open it up to experience it all.

introspection

sun drunk
sharing salt
between our lips
summer lust
never tasted
so sweet

ellie halo

your lips taste like an adventure
i want to dive right in

introspection

when the universe
sends you adversity
it is teaching you
how to rise
with the stars

see hinderance
as an invitation
to take a new direction

soon you will see
the barricades built
using your triggers as framework
were only there to protect
your greatest good

ellie halo

what are you being called to rise from?

introspection

dominate your ego
with integrity for self
know that anger is born
through years of repression
or opposing passion

make room for love
by evicting the angst
for it has no place
finding shelter
on the left side
of your chest

strip yourself bare
from built up rage
find comfort in compassion
while foraging through
your overgrown sorrows

ellie halo

warmth aids resentment
so light the fire
between surrender
and temper
until you are left
with debris

introspection

harbour anger
into advocacy
for the change
you wish to see

ellie halo

your anger will not heal the world.
transmute aggression into advocacy
and watch the revolution unfold.

introspection

we must award the rain
equal praise to the sun

for the dance between
flora and fauna
is what keeps
this world
turning

ellie halo

embrace every season.

introspection

cherries and tempranillo
leaving carmine stains
in the inside of my lips
matching my blushed cheeks
from smiling too much

the beauty
of the drowning sun
enriches my mood
accompanied by you
and a glass or two
of your finest wine

ellie halo

– sunsets on the porch

introspection

love is my true north;
the compass i use to navigate
the unfolding of destiny

when thunder crashes down
obliterating my path
i put my hands upon my heart
and ask to be guided home
back to my centre
of solitude

ellie halo

*i ask the universe to guide me.
i trust that all is working
in my highest favour.*

introspection

for a star
to soften it's shine
in an attempt to accommodate
for the moon's distress
is a universal tragedy

there is space
for both to emanate
their own flare

ellie halo

*you don't have to dim your light
so someone else can shine.*

introspection

promise me
that you will never
make yourself smaller
to ease the pain of another

their shortcomings
are not yours
to cater to

their projections
are not yours
to mirror

ellie halo

*to shrink yourself
for being too much
is a crime against
humanity.*

introspection

your passion lives
in your dreamy sleep state
when concepts flood
your entire body
creating magic
in the space
between your head
and heart

follow your highest vision
through and through and through
disregard sense or rationality
or the fears of those around you

this dream is yours
to bring to fruition
lean into your intuition
close your eyes
and just listen

ellie halo

*you are worthy of waking
your dreams into reality.*

introspection

there she is
looking back at me
mesmerised
by her tenacity
and influence

the woman that fought
for her wildest ambitions
and did not let
the opinions of others
discourage her desires
to make something
of her self

she made a promise
to her younger self
and here she is
living proof

ellie halo

*i choose to give power
to the ambition within me.
this life is mine to endlessly create.*

introspection

feel the hum of your heart
delicate simplicity
wrapped in armour
working hard with ease

breathe into the space
that allows you to feel
the force of fresh air
soaking your lungs
in sweet equanimity

ellie halo

stop.
breathe.
listen.

introspection

do not lose hope
while searching
for your roots

there is always
a place for you here

no matter your gender
or the way you make a living
your income bracket
or the person that you're kissing

there is always
space for you here

no matter your struggles
or the past of your sins
your ethnicity or background
or the colour of your skin

there is always
a place for you here

ellie halo

- we all belong here

introspection

transmute comparison
into celebration
of individuality

ellie halo

who are you comparing yourself to?

how can you celebrate your authenticity?

introspection

seek understanding over judgement

criticism is unfamiliarity;
a fear of what is not known

ellie halo

we judge what we do not understand.

introspection

dress yourself
with botanics and linen
bless yourself
with space to listen
caress yourself
in your own vision
find self love
in the depths of your despair
seek acceptance
through a ritualistic prayer
and open your heart
to a whole new world out there

ellie halo

*treat yourself
like the goddess you are.*

introspection

freedom
is a birthright

don't hide away
from your liberty
to live a life
of pure pleasure
and heart bursting
sensation

ellie halo

find the courage
to go against the grain
with unshakeable audacity
to live in alignment
with all that you are

for you are free
to truly exceed
beyond the norm

introspection

"you don't need to know
what your heart doesn't involve"

ellie halo

– passed down words of wisdom

introspection

constant evaluation
and deep introspection
creates motion
towards true alignment

ellie halo

*are you moving closer to true alignment
with your soul?*

introspection

be where you are
right in this moment
shed the layers
of the subconscious mind
and become deeply aware
in this time and space

presence
is like gold
potent and priceless

ellie halo

*i am showing up with presence
right in this very moment.
i bring awareness
to this current time and space,
creating inner tranquility.*

introspection

the polarity
of the sun and moon
one rising
while the other falls
is the perfect analogy
for love and fear

follow your highest excitement
and watch the tension dissolve
for love and fear
cannot mutually exist
in the same moment

ellie halo

rise above fear through love.

introspection

sunshine on skin
warm like a hug
early rises
hot coffee in my mug
good morning text messages
make my heart smile
the smallest gestures
are always worthwhile
ocean swims
honest conversation
when the mind is open
there is space for elevation
chasing sunsets
as if it's the last day on earth
sleeping with the moon
rising to a full rebirth
honouring myself
trusting my intuition
making space
for my dreams
to come into fruition

ellie halo

see life is magic
if you choose it to be

open your eyes wide enough
and that you will see

introspection

i was made
to climb mountains
and exercise my lungs
to see just how far
my words can travel

ellie halo

i am liberating my voice.

introspection

unhealed scars
embedded in our skin
exposing the lineage
of our ancestral trauma
carried down through birth
woman to child

it is the agony
that sits heavy on our chests
when we suppress
our intuitive connection
to source

it is the labour practiced
in the name of service
even when our eyelids
cry the symphony
of sacrifice

it is the unsettling ache of discomfort
imposed through failed attempts
to be perfect in all forms
striving to be worth
something

ellie halo

it is time we join hands
and watch our wounds dissolve
amongst the bonfire
as we sing songs
commemorating our freedom
spawned from the exertion
of our sisters

introspection

an embodied woman
follows her inner guidance
releasing resistance
trusting her divine path

she is empowered
by her own unique beauty
knowing that her existence
is a rarity in itself

she stands in her truth
even if it means standing alone
rejecting pressure and performance
rediscovering her natural flow

she honours her needs
sets boundaries with ease
and protects her sacred energy

she finds her way back
to the nature of her existence
syncing up with the earth,
the moon and the stars

ellie halo

she gifts herself the space
to grow, to heal, to expand
offering up permission
for others to do the same

she is a golden light
illuminating
from the inside out
finding strength
in her sovereignty

she truly knows
that being herself
is the most powerful
thing she can be

introspection

i have taken
many trips
around the sun
each time rediscovering
a piece of me
that had been left behind
when parting the womb

i am not growing
i am returning
to my fullness

ellie halo

– forever finding my way back home

introspection

to the women
who cracked me open
with insights
beyond my horizon
who showed me courage
through vulnerability
and self reclamation
through reckless devotion
i cherish you
and the space you hold
for the rising
of the divine feminine

ellie halo

may she be liberated
from internalised misogyny
and empowered
by her own autonomy

expanding her wings
in the midst of a cyclone
trusting herself
to navigate
her way back home

i hope these words ignite your soul
& guide you to find your light

where you can be seen,
in all your glory

forever grateful for —

g'ma.
you're a reminder of how resilient this lineage of women are. thank you for gifting me my first book of poetry and initiating this journey.

ma.
you have shown me what unconditional love truly means. thank you for believing in me since birth. i would not be here without your endless support.

dad.
through adversity and ease, we stand stronger than ever. i'm so grateful to have you as a part of me.

jack.
thank you for teaching me how to be brave. you will never know just how much you mean to me.

mietta.
you make me feel like anything is possible. thank you for giving me the gift of true sisterhood.

lily.
you inspire me every single day. thank you for being you.

my girls.
you know who you are. thank you for seeing me in my entirety. your love is what keeps my world turning.

my community.
the people who have continued to show up. your presence makes me feel like the luckiest girl in the world. thank you for being here with me.

Introspection © 2021
Copyright by Ellie Halo.
All rights reserved.

Self Published.
hello@elliehalo.com.au

This book contains material protected under International and Federal Copyright Laws and Treaties. Any unauthorised reprint or use of this material is prohibited. No part of this book may be reproduced or transmitted in any form or by any means, electronic or mechanical, including photocopying, recording, or by any information storage and retrieval system without express written permission from the author or publisher.

Paperback ISBN: 978-0-646-83704-8
eBook ISBN: 978-0-646-83731-4

www.ingramcontent.com/pod-product-compliance
Lightning Source LLC
Chambersburg PA
CBHW020314010526
44107CB00054B/1833